MYTHICAL CREATURES
DRAGONS

BY LISA OWINGS

BELLWETHER MEDIA • MINNEAPOLIS, MN

Torque brims with excitement perfect for thrill-seekers of all kinds. Discover daring survival skills, explore uncharted worlds, and marvel at mighty engines and extreme sports. In *Torque* books, anything can happen. Are you ready?

This edition first published in 2021 by Bellwether Media, Inc.

No part of this publication may be reproduced in whole or in part without written permission of the publisher.
For information regarding permission, write to Bellwether Media, Inc., Attention: Permissions Department,
6012 Blue Circle Drive, Minnetonka, MN 55343.

Library of Congress Cataloging-in-Publication Data

Names: Owings, Lisa, author.
Title: Dragons / by Lisa Owings.
Description: Minneapolis, MN : Bellwether Media, Inc., [2021] | Series: Torque: mythical creatures | Includes bibliographical references and index. | Audience: Ages 7-12 | Audience: Grades 4-6 | Summary: "Engaging images accompany information about dragons. The combination of high-interest subject matter and light text is intended for students in grades 3 through 7"- Provided by publisher.
Identifiers: LCCN 2020014861 (print) | LCCN 2020014862 (ebook) | ISBN 9781644872734 (library binding) | ISBN 9781681037363 (ebook)
Subjects: LCSH: Dragons–Juvenile literature. | Animals, Mythical–Juvenile literature.
Classification: LCC GR830.D7 O95 2021 (print) | LCC GR830.D7 (ebook) | DDC 398/.469–dc23
LC record available at https://lccn.loc.gov/2020014861
LC ebook record available at https://lccn.loc.gov/2020014862

Text copyright © 2021 by Bellwether Media, Inc. TORQUE and associated logos are trademarks and/or registered trademarks of Bellwether Media, Inc.

Editor: Rebecca Sabelko   Designer: Josh Brink

Printed in the United States of America, North Mankato, MN.

TABLE OF CONTENTS

BEASTS OF FLAME	4
FROM SERPENTS TO MONSTERS	10
FRIEND AND FOE	18
GLOSSARY	22
TO LEARN MORE	23
INDEX	24

BEASTS OF FLAME

Two dragons flap their bat-like wings and soar over a **remote** village. The townspeople watch in horror as the dragons breathe flames over the roofs.

The dragons' tails snake above the trees as they make their way back to their **lair**. The beasts curl around their pile of gold and sleep.

Treasure Guardians

Many dragons are said to spend their lives guarding piles of riches. Some attack humans who dare to steal their treasure. Others give gifts to worthy humans.

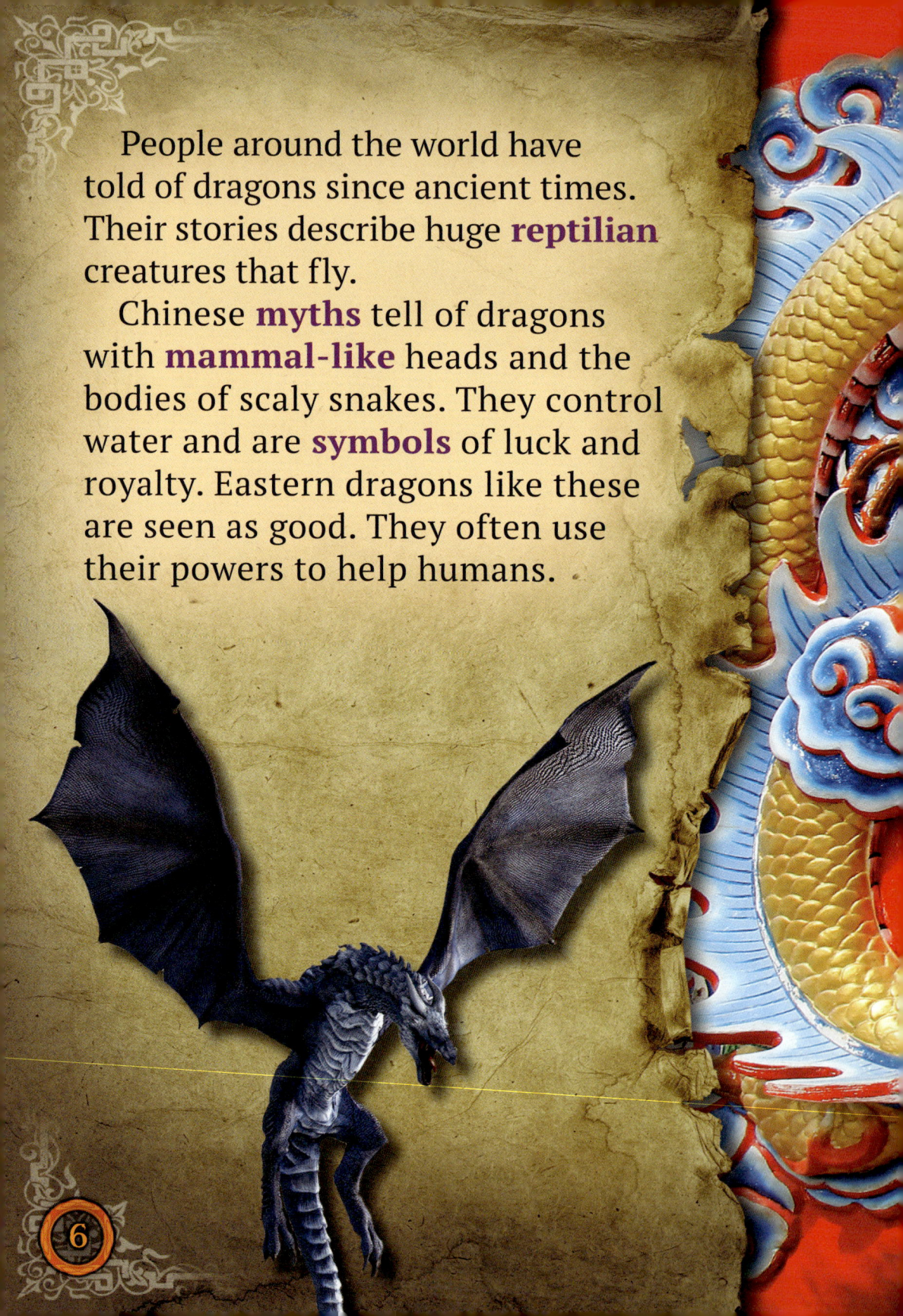

People around the world have told of dragons since ancient times. Their stories describe huge **reptilian** creatures that fly.

Chinese **myths** tell of dragons with **mammal-like** heads and the bodies of scaly snakes. They control water and are **symbols** of luck and royalty. Eastern dragons like these are seen as good. They often use their powers to help humans.

BABY DRAGONS
Like other baby reptiles, dragons are said to hatch from eggs. They often need fire to hatch. In some myths, they emerge as tiny worms.

Saint George and the Dragon

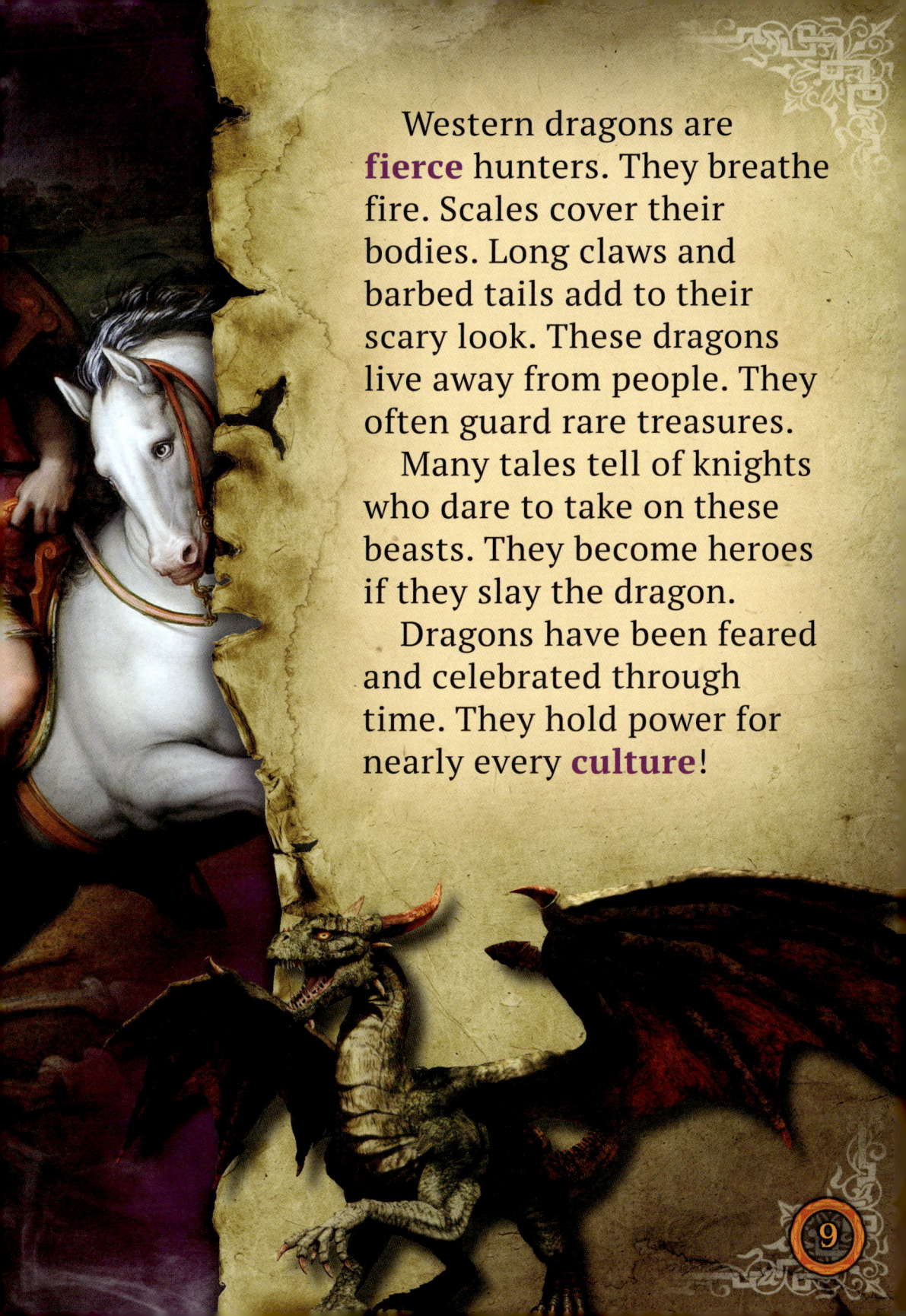

Western dragons are **fierce** hunters. They breathe fire. Scales cover their bodies. Long claws and barbed tails add to their scary look. These dragons live away from people. They often guard rare treasures.

Many tales tell of knights who dare to take on these beasts. They become heroes if they slay the dragon.

Dragons have been feared and celebrated through time. They hold power for nearly every **culture**!

FROM SERPENTS TO MONSTERS

Many cultures have dragon myths. The earliest dragons go back to at least 4000 BCE. They looked like giant snakes. Many had no wings.

Dragon Origin

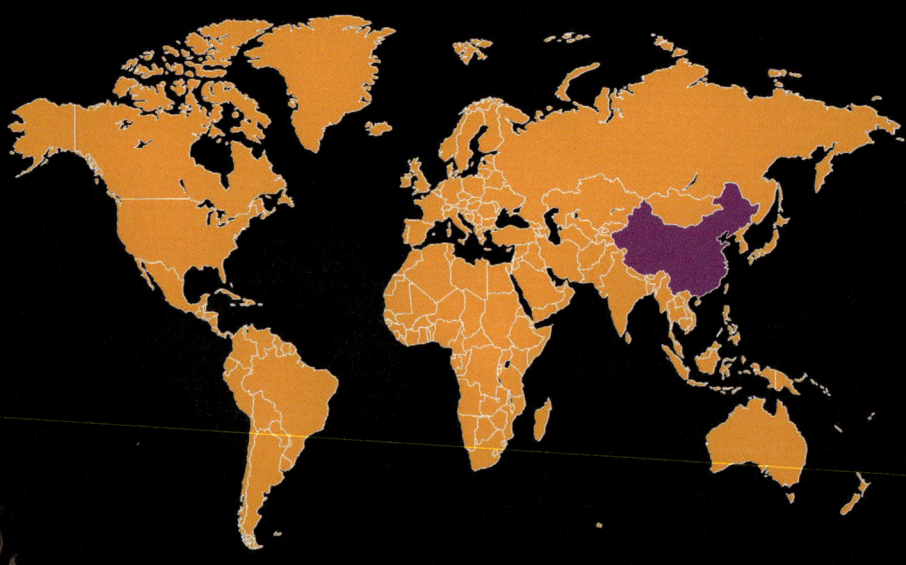

China = ◼

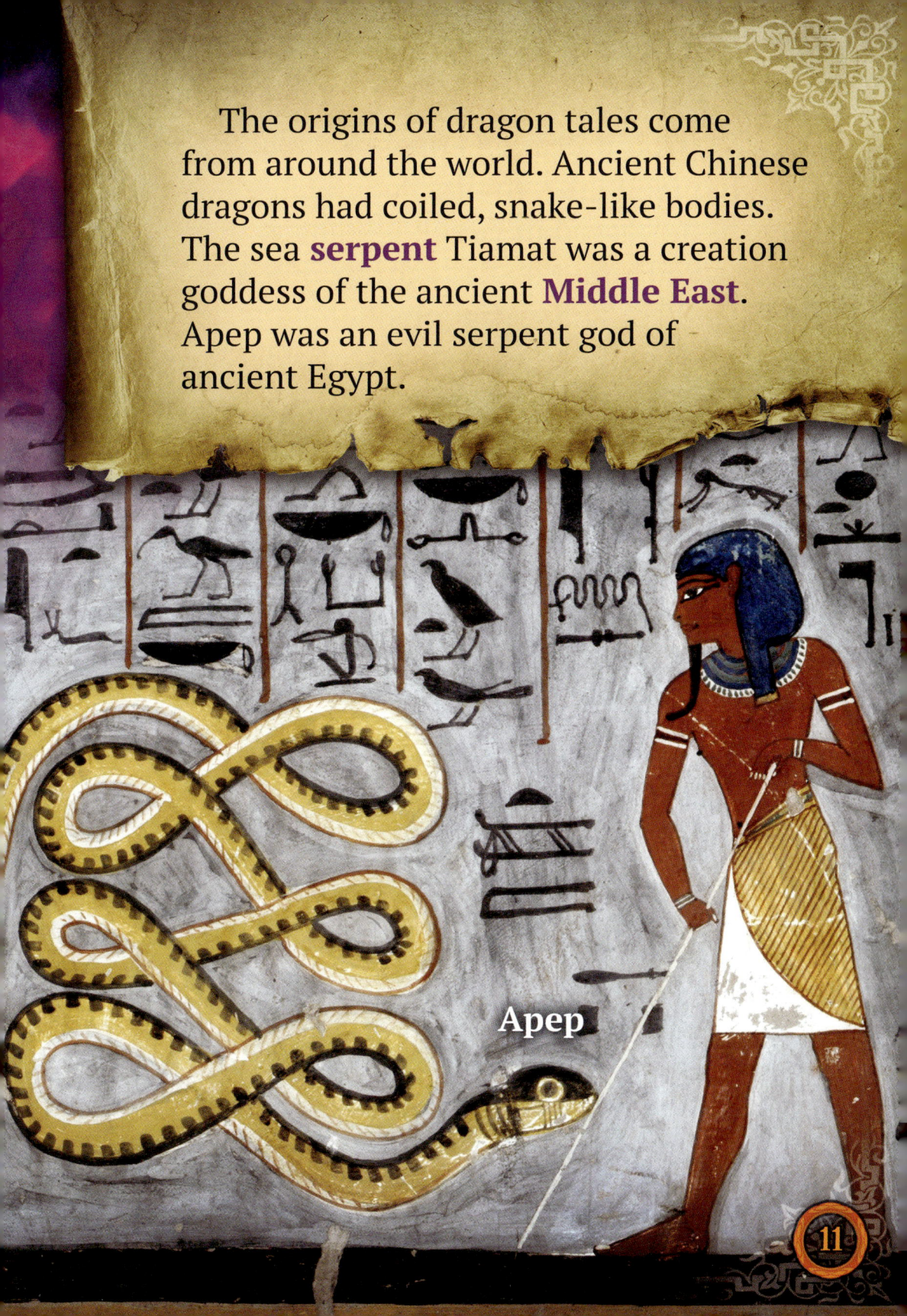

The origins of dragon tales come from around the world. Ancient Chinese dragons had coiled, snake-like bodies. The sea **serpent** Tiamat was a creation goddess of the ancient **Middle East**. Apep was an evil serpent god of ancient Egypt.

Apep

Early serpent dragons may have **inspired** later myths. Dragons appeared in Greek stories like Homer's *Iliad* during the 700s BCE. These dragons sometimes had wings or many heads. They were fierce but not evil. They often served the gods and guarded treasures.

Chinese dragons were seen as kind and just. Many **emperors**, such as Emperor Taizong, held close ties to them.

Emperor Taizong

Dragon Timeline

Around 4000 BCE: Serpent dragons appear in Chinese art

700s BCE: Homer's *Iliad* describes a dragon figure on the king's shield

Around 800 CE: A hero fights a dragon in the Old English epic poem *Beowulf*

Dragons of the East and West

	East	West
brings fortune and rain		
evil, fire breathing		
can fly		
has scales, horns, claws		
guards treasure		

During the **Middle Ages**, western dragons became feared creatures. They took on wings, fiery breath, and bad tempers. Dragons were linked to the evil serpent in the Bible as Christianity spread. Stories like *Beowulf* celebrated dragons' downfall.

But eastern dragons continued to bring luck, wisdom, and rain. They flew without wings. **Antlers** and fur made their heads less snakelike. They often changed shape or size.

eastern dragon

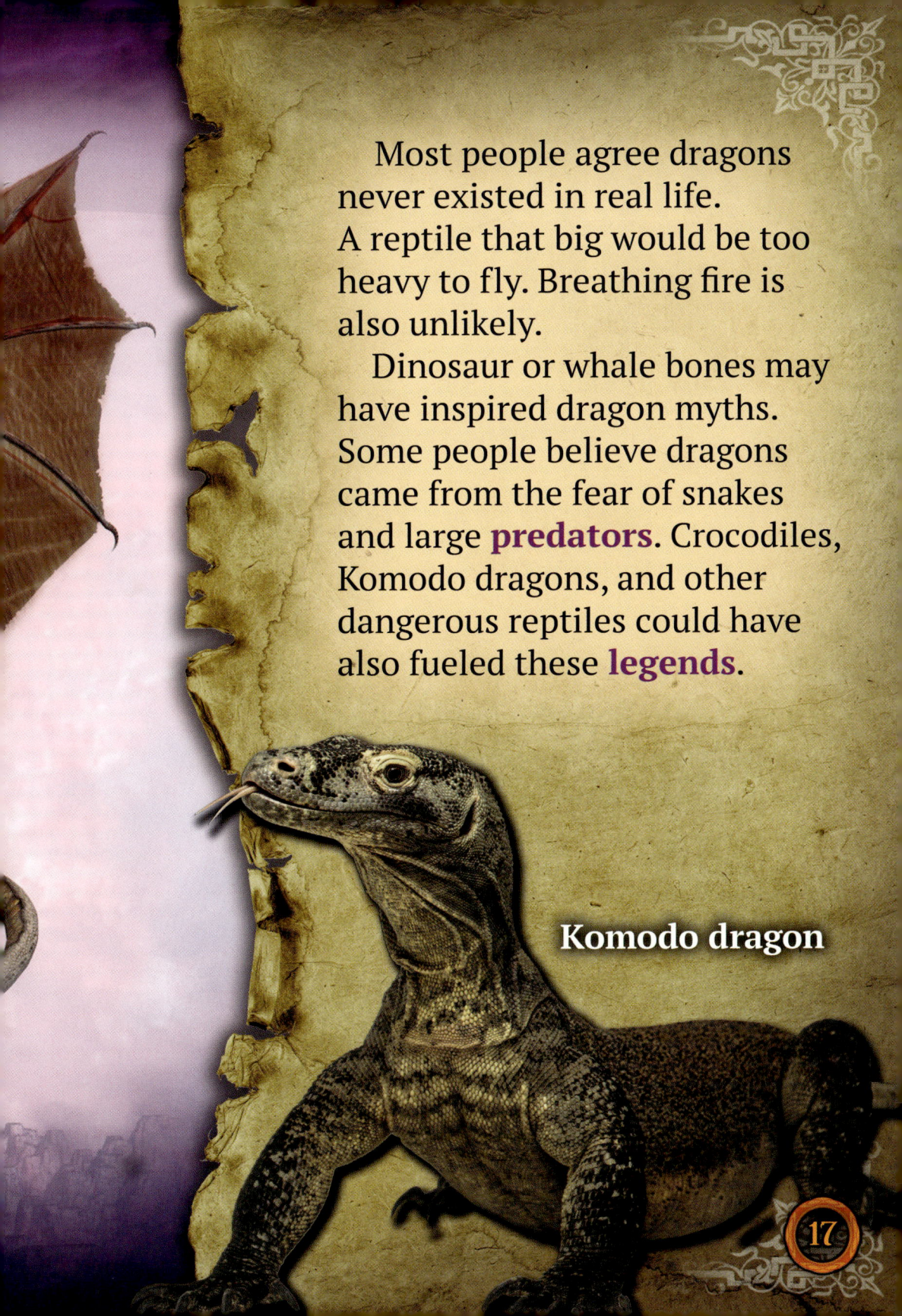

Most people agree dragons never existed in real life. A reptile that big would be too heavy to fly. Breathing fire is also unlikely.

Dinosaur or whale bones may have inspired dragon myths. Some people believe dragons came from the fear of snakes and large **predators**. Crocodiles, Komodo dragons, and other dangerous reptiles could have also fueled these **legends**.

Komodo dragon

FRIEND AND FOE

Western dragons are still seen as huge fire-breathing reptiles that fly. They can be any color. Each dragon can have different traits or powers.

Common powers include changing shape and reading people's thoughts. Some modern dragons are cruel, like J.R.R. Tolkien's Smaug. They burn or eat anything in their path.

Harry Potter Dragons

Many dragons appear in the Harry Potter series. Harry has to battle a nasty dragon in *Harry Potter and the Goblet of Fire*. He flies on his broom to avoid getting burned.

Smaug

How to Train Your Dragon

Today's dragons often help humans. Stories such as *Eragon* tell of humans caring for these beasts. The How to Train Your Dragon films show dragons' friendly sides.

Media Mention

Movie: *Spirited Away*

Year Released: 2001

Character: Haku, a dragon spirit disguised as a boy who helps Chihiro escape the spirit world

Powers: flies, casts spells, moves objects with mind, places memories in others' minds, uses a force field

Eastern dragons remain symbols of luck, wisdom, and strength. Dragon dances are performed in China. Dancers use poles to bring colorful fabric dragons to life. All around the world, dragons still soar through our imaginations!

GLOSSARY

antlers—branched bones on the heads of some animals; antlers often look like horns.

culture—the beliefs, values, and ways of life of a group of people

emperors—male rulers of a group of countries or states; emperors once ruled China.

fierce—strong and intense

inspired—gave someone an idea about what to do or create

lair—the resting place of a wild animal

legends—stories from the past that are believed by many people but cannot be proved to be true

mammal-like—similar to warm-blooded animals that have backbones and feed their young milk

Middle Ages—the period of European history from about 500 to 1500 CE

Middle East—a region of southwestern Asia and northern Africa; this region includes Egypt, Lebanon, Iran, Iraq, Israel, Saudi Arabia, Syria, and other nearby countries.

myths—ancient stories about the beliefs or history of a group of people; myths also try to explain events.

predators—animals that hunt other animals for food

remote—far away from others

reptilian—having the traits of cold-blooded animals that have backbones and lay eggs

serpent—a large snake

symbols—things that stand for something else

TO LEARN MORE

AT THE LIBRARY

Lawrence, Sandra, and Stuart Hill. *The Atlas of Monsters: Mythical Creatures from Around the World.* Philadelphia, Pa.: Running Press Kids, 2019.

London, Martha. *Dragons.* Minneapolis, Minn.: Pop!, 2020.

Mason, Jennifer. *Dragon Myths.* New York, N.Y.: Gareth Stevens Publishing, 2018.

ON THE WEB

FACTSURFER

Factsurfer.com gives you a safe, fun way to find more information.

1. Go to www.factsurfer.com

2. Enter "dragons" into the search box and click 🔍.

3. Select your book cover to see a list of related content.

INDEX

Apep, 11
appearance, 4, 6, 9, 10, 11, 12, 14, 15, 18
Beowulf, 14
Bible, 14
China, 6, 10, 11, 12, 21
Christianity, 14
culture, 9, 10
eastern dragons, 6, 14, 15, 21
Egypt, 11
Emperor Taizong, 12
emperors, 12
Eragon, 20
explanations, 17
fire, 4, 8, 9, 14, 17, 18
fly, 6, 15, 17, 18
Harry Potter, 18
history, 10, 11, 12, 14
How to Train Your Dragon (series), 20
humans, 5, 6, 20
Iliad, 12
legends, 17
Middle Ages, 14
Middle East, 11
myths, 6, 8, 10, 12, 17
origins, 10, 11
powers, 6, 18
reptiles, 6, 8, 17, 18
serpent, 11, 12, 14
Smaug, 18, 19
Spirited Away, 21
symbols, 6, 21
Tiamat, 11
timeline, 12-13
Tolkien, J.R.R., 18
treasure, 4, 5, 9, 12
western dragons, 9, 14, 18
wings, 4, 10, 12, 14, 15

The images in this book are reproduced through the courtesy of: DM7, front cover (hero); JekLi, front cover (background); easy camera, pp. 2-3 (background), 22-23 (background), 24 (background); Valentyna Chukhlyebova, p. 3; Melkor3D, pp. 4, 4-5; Dream Expander, p. 6; Patthawan Supjaroentawee, pp. 6-7; Album/ Alamy, pp. 8-9; Warpaint, p. 9; De Agostinini/ S. Vannini/ Newscom, pp. 10-11; Imaginechina-Tuchong/ Alamy, p. 12; nopira/ Wiki Commons, p. 13 (top); JW1805/ Wiki Commons, p. 13 (middle); Ivy Close Images/ Alamy, p. 13 (bottom); david sanger photography/ Alamy, pp. 14-15; Elena Elenaphotos21/ Alamy, pp. 16-17; Eric Isselee, p. 17; Allstar Picture Library/ Alamy, pp. 18-19, 20-21, 22; tsuneomp, p. 23.